If Gumdrops
Fell Like Raindrops...

A Collection of Poems

Enjoy!
Thalia Marakas

If Gumdrops
Fell Like Raindrops...

A Collection of Poems

Written by Thalia Marakas • Illustrated by Ben Griffin

TM Publishing • Connecticut

TM Publishing, a division of
TM Enterprises, LLC
P.O. Box 1183
Ridgefield, Connecticut 06877

Library of Congress Cataloging-in-Publication Data: 00-191259

Marakas, Thalia

If gumdrops fell like raindrops...a collection of poems / written by Thalia Marakas; illustrated by Ben Griffin

Summary: Take a journey through the times and memories of childhood.
New poems to remind everyone of the joys and trials of growing up.

ISBN 0-9676258-1-5

Book designed by Denise Hearon, Design House Advertising
Ridgefield, Connecticut

Published in Connecticut by TM Publishing, a division of TM Enterprises, LLC
Book Title and Publisher's logo are trademarks of TM Enterprises, LLC

10 9 8 7 6 5 4 3 2

Printing: Modern International Graphics, Inc., Eastlake, Ohio

Underneath the ocean waves
Live creatures of the sea.
Hop aboard a submarine;
Explore the deep with me.

And when we've seen the ocean,
We'll take a trip through space.
Hop aboard a rocket ship;
Observe earth's changing face.

Look at life through windows;
Enjoy the view and see
A world of fascination.
Won't you look with me?

WITH APPRECIATION AND HEARTFELT THANKS

To my late parents, John and Katherine Emanuel, for instilling in me the importance of hard work and perseverance, for showing me that all experiences, good and bad, are learning opportunities, and for making sure I grew up knowing what really matters in life.

To my beloved late husband, George Marakas, for his deep devotion and commitment to family, great strength and dignity, phenomenal sense of humor, and most of all, his love.

To my daughter, Vanessa, and my son, Nick, who were the inspirations for many of my poems. They have brought me much joy and have always made me proud. I could not have accomplished this without their love and support and their invaluable input and insight.

To all my relatives and friends for their kind words of encouragement, belief in me, and for allowing me to use their names throughout the book!

To Bill Whittemore, my attorney and friend; to Gail Eltringham and Deeny Bennett for their editing; to my art director, Denise Hearon at Design House Advertising; and of course to Ben, without whom this book would not have been possible.

—Thalia

TABLE OF CONTENTS

Gumdrops 1

Inside a Purse 2

Rain and Puddles 4

Daffodils 5

A Leprechaun 6

My Mom Just Had a Baby 8

I'm Adopted 10

Joey and Leah 11

Mindy, Megan, and Maribel 12

Easter 13

Ballerina Maria 14

Arlene Christine 16

The Circus 18

Dear Dad 20

Nicholas Jonathan George 22

Nate the Snake 24

Snakes, Lizards, Mice, and Toads ...25

Centipedes 26

Leon the Chameleon 28

Ice Cream 30

Floating on a Cloud 31

When I Grow Up 32

Amy's Allergies 34

My Pet Died 35

A Name for My Pet 36

Families 38

I Hate School, Sooo... 40

I Am Not You and You Are Not Me 42

I Want My Teacher Fired 44

A Cause for Celebration 46

Melinda's Tonsils 48

Stanley, David, and Marina Renée 49

Someone Will Take Care of You 50

Balloons of Many Colors 52

Sunset and Sunrise 54

What's This Green Thing? 56

One of a Kind 58

My Friend Dee 60

Brothers! 62

We 64

Stella's Dilemma 66

Differences 68

A Family Dinner 70

Lollipops 72

Christmas and Hanukkah 74

Snowflakes 76

No TV? 78

Story Time 80

"WILSON"

Created by Ben Griffin during his doodling days in high school, the character Wilson is found in each illustration accompanying the poems in this book. Wilson was created with the intent of being a character with no outstanding look, one with whom everyone can identify. On every page, you can find Wilson in lively artwork exemplifying rich imagination.

GUMDROPS

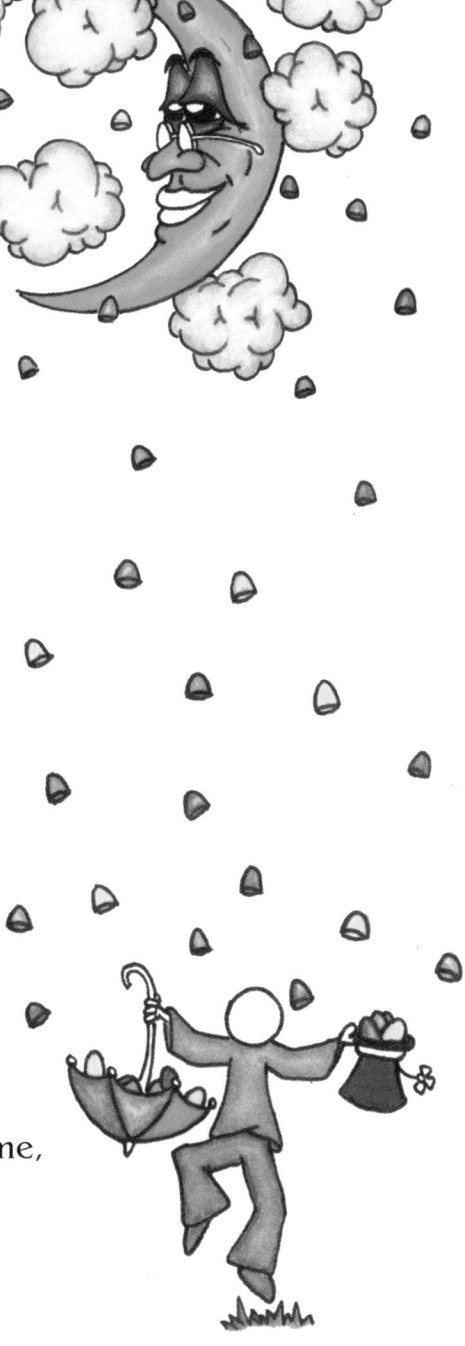

If gumdrops fell like raindrops,
Wouldn't it be a treat?
No raincoats on our bodies;
No galoshes on our feet!

But we could use umbrellas,
And turn them upside down
To catch the many gumdrops,
Before they'd hit the ground!

If gumdrops fell like raindrops,
Would grass and flowers grow?
And would they change the colors
Of streams and frogs and snow?

"Just a few more questions,"
I said to Mom and Dad,
Who shook their heads and asked me,
"What made you think of that?"

1

INSIDE A PURSE

I've often wondered what could be worse
Than figuring out what to keep in my purse!

Something to eat——'cause I can get hungry,
A comb, a mirror, and, of course, some money.
In case of a power failure somewhere,
A flashlight or two and I'll be prepared.
Pencils and paper——I ALWAYS get bored.
My telephone books and quarters galore!
If there's lots of time to spare,
A pack of cards to play solitaire.
A book to read and keys to my house,
My brother's drawing of a mouse.
Notes and letters from my friends,
Extra Kleenexes to lend.

A stapler always comes in handy...
M & M's——my favorite candy!
Eye shadow, lipstick, powder, and blush,
Tape player, tapes, my grandmother's watch,
Nail polish, jewelry, and library card,
   A paper clip, a good luck charm,
      Two video games, AND
         Five packs of gum!

         Oh well, next time I'll REALLY decide.
            For now, all this stuff——
               Goes right back inside!!

3

RAIN AND PUDDLES

Ain't it great when it rains?
We can have fun for hours.
All we gotta do—
Is jump in all the puddles!

DAFFODILS

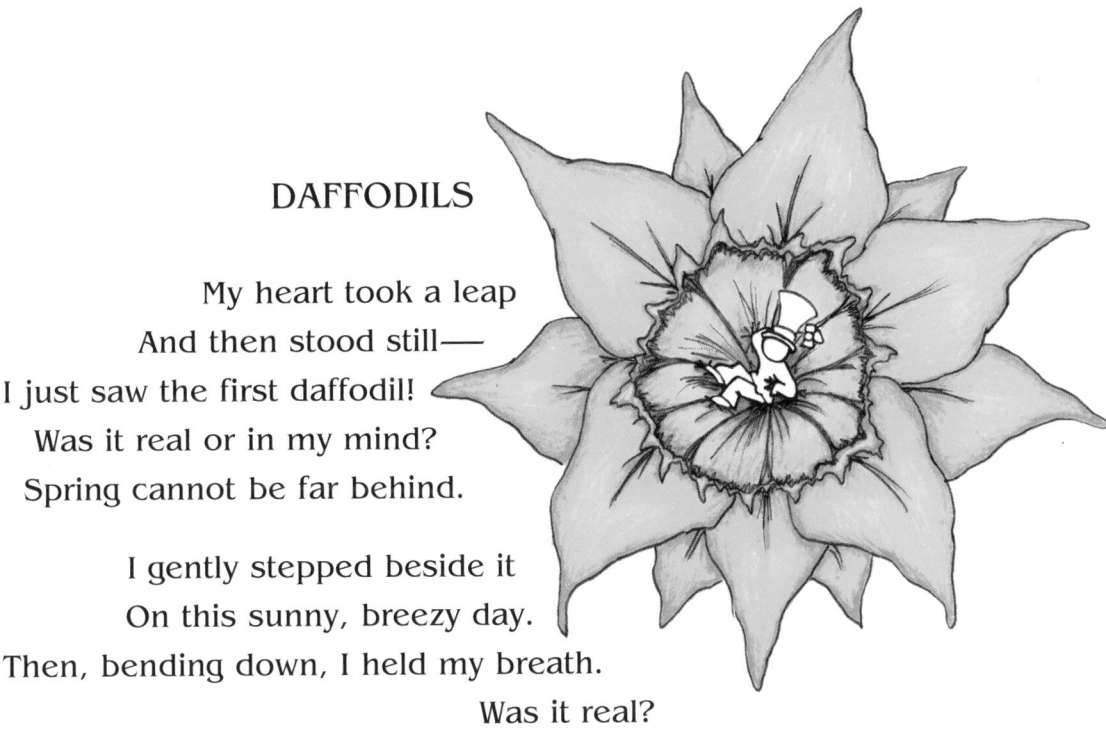

My heart took a leap
And then stood still—
I just saw the first daffodil!
Was it real or in my mind?
Spring cannot be far behind.

I gently stepped beside it
On this sunny, breezy day.
Then, bending down, I held my breath.
Was it real?
Ahhh...YESSS...!!

A LEPRECHAUN

Flying on an airplane,
Bored as bored can be,
I looked outside my window,
And guess what I did see?

A leprechaun was sitting,
Still as he could be,
Sitting on the silver wing,
Smiling up at me.

Flight attendants walked on by.
I guess they did not see
The mischievous wee leprechaun
Smiling up at me.

I thought that I was dreaming.
A feat (Wouldn't you agree?)—
Sitting on an airplane's wing,
Still as still can be.

I gave a little smile back,
Wondering what he'd do.
That's when he flashed his sign up high:
HAPPY ST. PATRICK'S DAY TO YOU!

MY MOM JUST HAD A BABY!

My mom just had a baby,
AND BOY WAS I UPSET!
I didn't feel like sharing
ANYTHING with him yet!
I didn't think that I was ready,
To share my life, my space.
I didn't think that I was ready,
And then I saw his face.
Wrapped in a flowered blanket,
Tiny as can be,
Wrapped in a flowered blanket,
Gazing right at me!

Well...maybe I can teach him
A couple things in life.
Since we have to keep him,
I guess I could be nice.
I'll teach him how to run,
And I'll teach him how to play.
I'll teach him other things, of course,
And guide him on his way.
I'll be the older child now,
And that shouldn't be too bad.
I'll be the smarter child now,
And that will be just GRAND!!

9

I'M ADOPTED

I know that I'm adopted—
My parents told me so.
I know how much they wanted me;
They've always let it show.
The happiness I've brought
Has given them a glow.
I cherish and adore them,
Because they love me so!

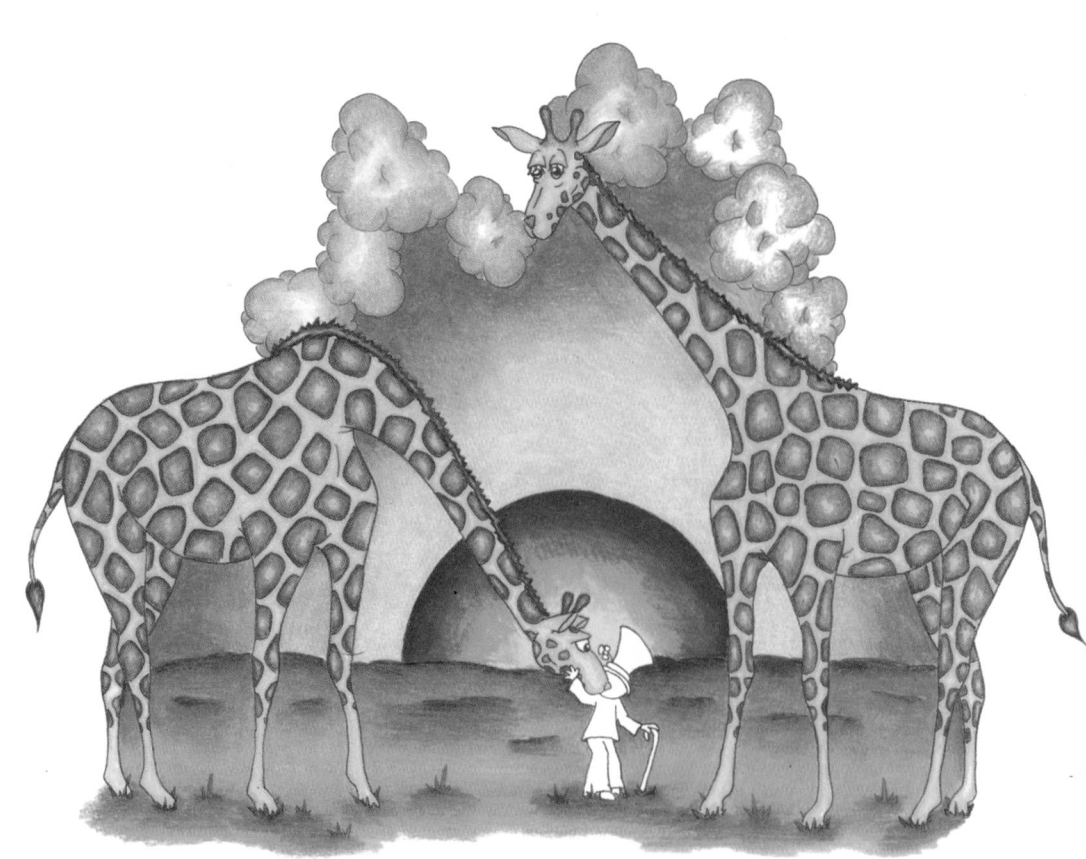

JOEY AND LEAH

Joey and Leah are an unusual pair;
He does chores while her spitballs fill the air.

He wants his clothes neatly pressed;
She plays in mud, wearing a dress.

He'll always be careful climbing a tree;
Somehow she'll manage to skin her knee.

He collects stamps and coins, and all sorts of cards;
She collects only grubs she finds in the yard.

He cleans out his room without delay;
She cleans out her room only in May.

They're totally different: Leah's night; Joey's day.
Yet brother and sister they always will stay!

MINDY, MEGAN, AND MARIBEL

I named my gerbil, hamster, and snail
Mindy, Megan, and Maribel.
At first they were Evan, Ed, and Earl—
Until I discovered that each was a girl!
When my sister gave these gifts to me,
I couldn't believe my luck.
And now I live with THREE MORE GIRLS.
YUCK!   YUCK!   YUCK!

EASTER

I found a bug,
A great BIG bug,
And gave it to my sister.
I watched her scream
And then pass out.
WHAT A HAPPY EASTER!!

BALLERINA MARIA

Ballerina Maria would dance on her toes
While eating a Popsicle and smelling a rose.
But that didn't impress me
As much as the monkey
Hanging on her knee!

She'd love to strike an unusual pose,
Recite some poetry, and wiggle her nose.
But this was not all Maria could do;
She could bend over backwards
AND tie her own shoe!

Her mom and dad would beg and beg,
"Maria, quit balancing things on your head!"
But she continued to dance on her toes
While eating her Popsicle
And smelling her rose.

16

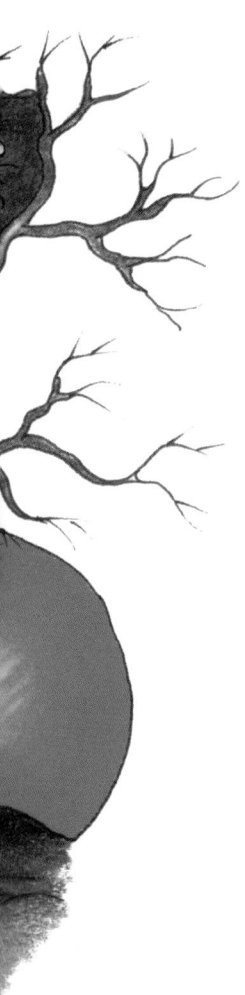

ARLENE CHRISTINE

Early one morning in New Orleans,
Arlene Christine decided to sing.
She started at breakfast
And sang right through lunch.
It was pretty amazing;
She didn't stop once!
She sang in the kitchen;
She sang on the couch;
She sang in her bedroom;
Throughout her whole house!
She didn't play; she didn't eat;
She never even went to sleep!
She sang opera; she sang soul;
She even sang rock and roll!
She sang country and the blues,
Jazz and rap and gospel, too!
And since that day she decided to sing,
All of her neighbors asked her one thing—
"Why did you have to choose New Orleans?!"

THE CIRCUS

Right side up, upside down,
Goes the circus clown.
Isn't it amazing
How he jumps around?

Over here, over there,
Smiling as he goes.
Don't you love his silly hats
And his funny clothes?

As I watch this circus act,
I'm glad as glad can be.
Going to the circus
Brings out the kid in me!

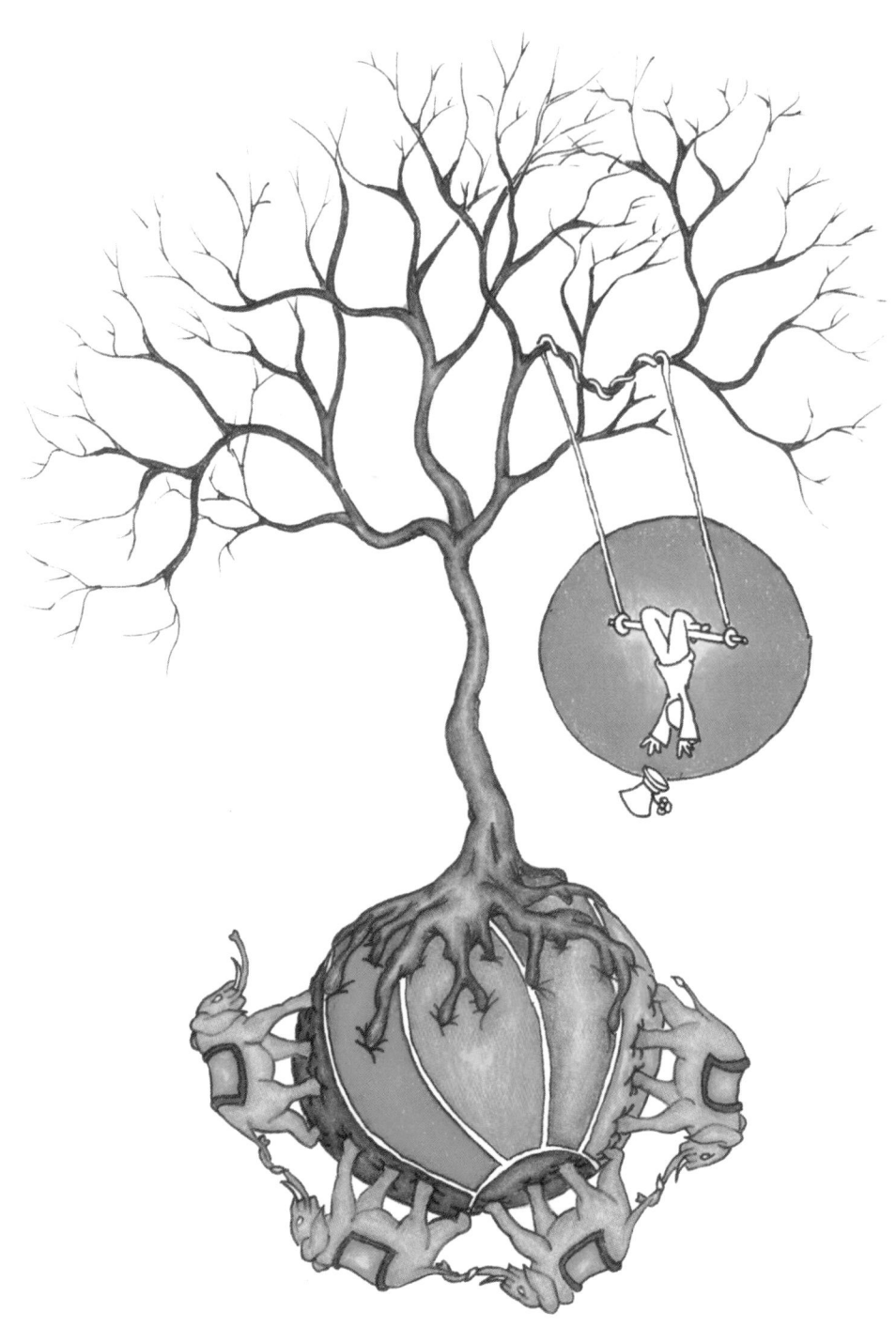

DEAR DAD

It doesn't bother you
When we make sculptures out of glue.
You don't lose your head
When we don't make our bed.

If we want to take some chances,
You don't give us worried glances.
And you know what's really nice?
If we ask, you'll give advice.

So by and by
And through and through—
Thanks a lot, Dad,
For all you do!

P.S. We love you...too!

NICHOLAS JONATHAN GEORGE

He closed his eyes and swung the bat
And hoped he'd hit the ball.
Then voices screamed from all around,
"GO, NICHOLAS, GO!!"
Quick as a wink he dropped the bat
And looking to tie the score
Thought, "Can I make it to first base—
Or maybe even home?"
Sure enough the ball did fly
Higher than the trees,
Over the head and through the hands
Of Michael Kalabreeze.
With open mouths all scratched their heads,
Unable to believe...
It was not too long ago
The others held the lead.

But now the kid with lots of faith
Had evened up the score!
His team shook hands, and said their thanks
To Nicholas Jonathan George.

22

NATE THE SNAKE

I asked my mom, quite innocently,
"May Nate, my pet, come live with me?"

"Yes," she laughed, then looked my way.
"Did you find another stray?"

Oops!

"Mom? Mom? You don't look great!
Should I have told you—Nate's a snake?"

"Sorry, Mom.
Please don't faint!!"

SNAKES, LIZARDS, MICE, AND TOADS

Snakes and lizards,
Mice and toads
Make up my collection
Of animals that need respect
And get no admiration.

Now I've heard others
Share my view;
That's my recollection.
I try explaining to my folks,
Who lack my fascination!

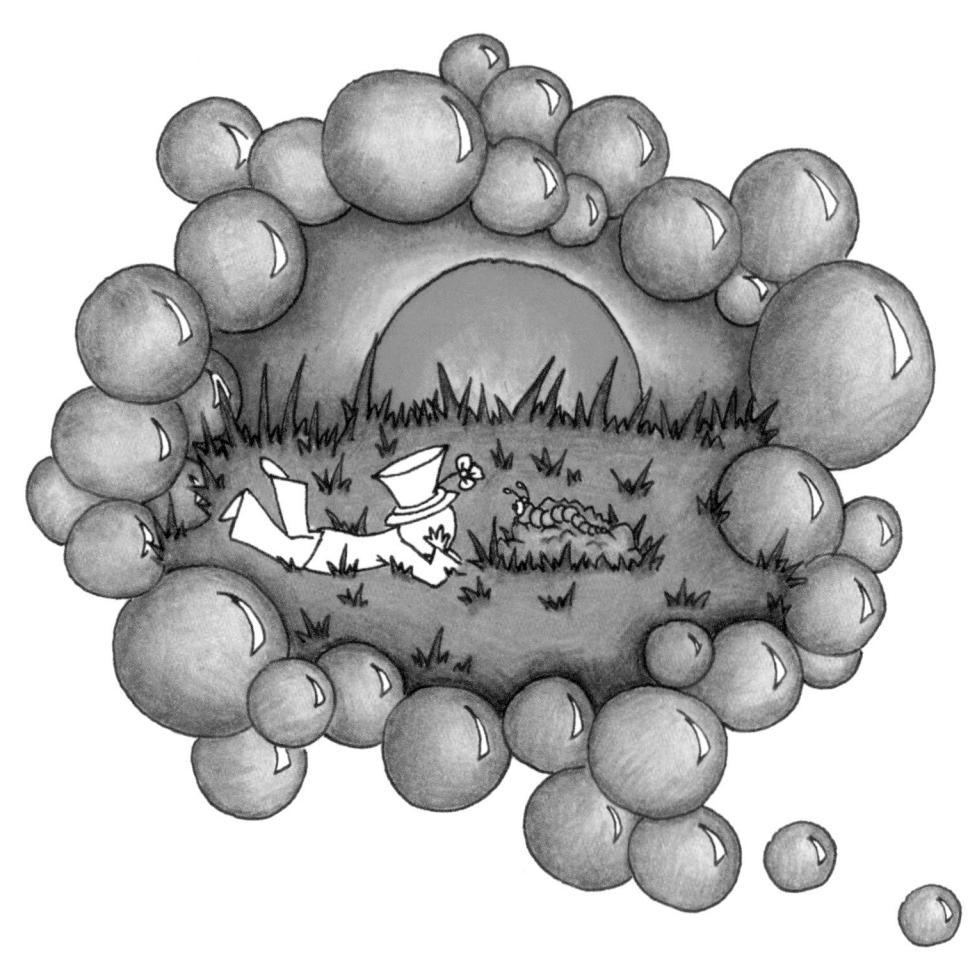

CENTIPEDES

Relax...Relaaax...
I told my mom.
I don't think you should holler.
Who could resist a centipede
FOR ONLY JUST A DOLLAR?

LEON THE CHAMELEON

Leon the chameleon was a funny little fellow.
Instead of turning green or brown,
He'd turn red or blue or yellow!
When he turned red, he'd hide in my bed.
When he turned blue, he'd hide in my shoe.
And when he turned yellow,
Well...
We'd all laugh and say,
"He sure is a funny little fellow!"

ICE CREAM

Quiver,
Shiver,
Down to the bone—
I just ate an ice cream cone!

Chocolate,
Vanilla,
Marshmallow Cream,
Strawberry,
Bubble Gum,
And Praline!

I wanted one scoop,
Then got carried away.
Six flavors, one price—
ONLY TODAY!

FLOATING ON A CLOUD

I'd love to float upon a cloud
And ponder this awhile:
What would it be like
To be a crocodile?

Would I miss my favorite cake
Or running barefoot by the lake?
Would I miss my friends at school
Or going swimming in a pool?

I know I'd miss my mom and dad
And all the happy times we've had.
I don't think that I could smile
If I were a crocodile.

I'd better float another mile
And ponder other things awhile...

WHEN I GROW UP

When I grow up, I want to be...
Just like the owl that sits in our tree.
It seems to me I've always heard
The owl is a wise old bird.

When I grow up, I want to be...
Just like the branches on our tree.
They can bend, it seems to me,
But do not break so easily.

When I grow up, I want to be...
Just like the flowers that grow on our tree.
From tiny buds, it seems to me,
They grow up very gracefully.

When I grow up, I want to be...
Just as sturdy as our tree.
It can change, it seems to me,
But always will remain a tree.

AMY'S ALLERGIES

Dogs and cats,
And rabbits, too.
Birds and milk
(To name a few).
Hamsters, horses,
Wool, and dust,
Pollen, mold—
Stay away she must.
Certain grasses,
Roses, too.
All these make her go
"AHHHCHOOO!!"

MY PET DIED

I had a pet,
And it died,
And I was very sad.
I cried and cried
For many days,
And I got
Really mad!

But then one day
I had a thought—
Why am I so mad?
Another pet
Will need a home,
And then I won't
Be sad!

So now, you see,
I'm busy
Looking for a pet.
And what about
The one that died?
Oh, I never
Will forget!

A NAME FOR MY PET

I asked the vet what to name my pet,
And here's what he said to me:
"Take this book and have a look.
It'll give you ideas—You'll see!"

Kaycee's an ant,
And Arthur's a worm.
A giraffe is named Allison;
Then there's Pano, the bird.

Mercedes, the dog,
And Chaz, the cat;
Michele is a fish,
And Jay is a bat.

Millie's a monkey,
And George is a squirrel;
A spider named Celia,
And a beetle named Merle.

James is a pig,
And Elisha's a yak;
Frosini's a camel.
How about that?

Stephanie's a deer,
And Kristin's a frog;
Mike's a gorilla
Who sits on a log!

Steve or Aggie?
Jonathan or Lee?
You could choose Effie
When naming your bee.

Lauren's a whale,
And Niki's an ox.
Donna or Elliott
Is ideal for a fox.

Starfish and clams—
Who should they be?
Lindsey or Ándrea
Or Sofia Marie?

Mary Ann is a mouse,
And Dean, an alligator.
I'm now out of time;
I'll continue reading later!!

FAMILIES

There are many types of families
Making up our world today.
And each one is unique
In its own particular way.

So yours and mine may differ——
Of course, that is okay.
And there may be confusion
In living day to day.

But one thing is for certain:
Clearly you can see
I really love my family,
And they really do love me!

I HATE SCHOOL, SOOO...

I'm sending in my resignation.
I need rest and relaxation!
I want a place that's far away—
Like Indonesia or Bombay!
Africa, perhaps, will do...
Ever been to Timbuktu?
Maybe I will choose Peru!

I've got to make my reservation.
What should be my destination?
The Orient's the place to go—
I've never been to Tokyo!
No one's there whom I will know!

No more time for vacillation.
No more thought or contemplation!
Any place will be okay.
School just opened—
Yesterday!

I AM NOT YOU AND YOU ARE NOT ME

I have trouble with my studies,
Understanding what I've read.
I have trouble writing numbers;
They're backwards in my head.
It may take me longer
To do what you do fast

Because——

I am not you,
And you are not me.

You and I are different,
In, oh, so many ways;
Yet you and I are similar,
So much you'd be amazed.

Remember——

I'd stand by you,
No matter what.
Would you stand by me,
No matter what?

Since——

I am not you,
And you are not me.
You're who you should be,
And I, of course, am ME!

I WANT MY TEACHER FIRED

I want my teacher fired;
I want her banned from school!
She told us we'd have fun this year—
That it would be really cool!

But now that we have started,
She's played a trick instead:
"We're going to learn to read and write!"
And that's not all she said.

"We've got to learn our numbers
And social studies, too.
Did I mention grammar?
What does science mean to you?"

I guess there'll be no fun this year—
Of this I was afraid.
I should have stayed in Kindergarten...
Do I really need First Grade?

A CAUSE FOR CELEBRATION

We're individuals. Let's celebrate!
We're each unique. Don't hesitate
To take a stand for your beliefs.
Be gracious in victory and defeat.

Be determined and stay strong—
We all have days when things go wrong.
And, if you don't like today,
Tomorrow's never far away.

Give life your all, and celebrate!
Be kind to others; you'll feel great!
There's always work that must be done.
We should do our part, each and every one.

Pick yourself up when you fall down,
'Cause no one else may be around.
And remember this one true fact:
We're each unique. What's better than that?

MELINDA'S TONSILS

Melinda yelled.
There was no doubt.
She did not want her tonsils out!
"Inside my throat,
Just hangin' there.
To pull them out—
Would that be fair?"

The doctor thought,
Then made a deal,
"You'll get ice cream at each meal!"
Melinda thought,
And then she said,
"Can I keep them...
By my bed?!"

STANLEY, DAVID, AND MARINA RENÉE

"Don't worry, we'll clean our rooms one day,"
Said Stanley, David, and Marina Renée.
"We'd surely do it right away,
Except our friends have come to play.
We would have done it yesterday,
Except it was a holiday.
Tomorrow it might be okay
If nothing else gets in the way."

And so it went, day after day,
Something always in the way.
Months soon passed, and years did, too.
The mess in their rooms just grew and grew!
They all left for college;
That day came too soon.
They all left for college—
Without cleaning their rooms!!

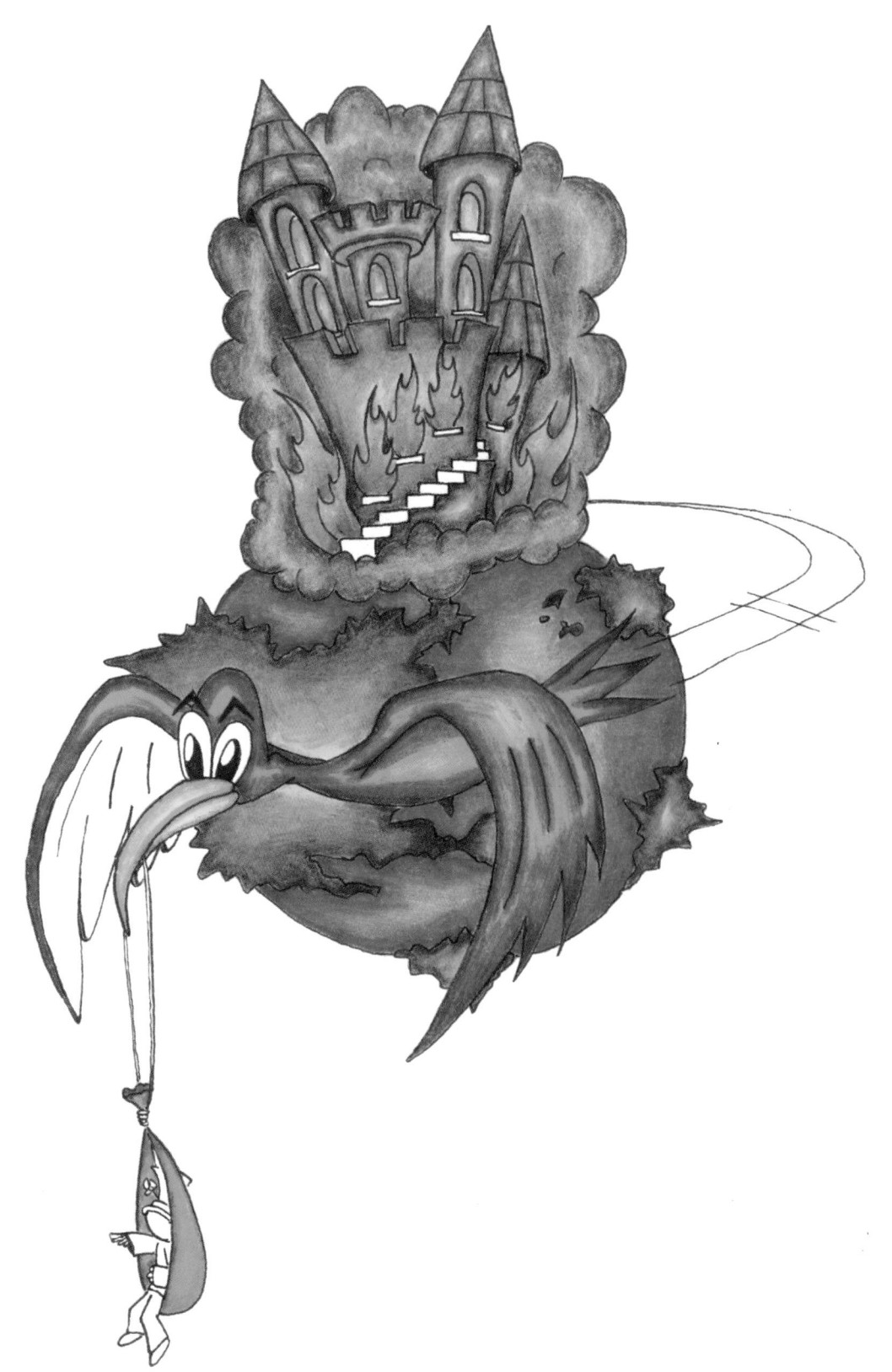

SOMEONE WILL TAKE CARE OF YOU

If you're depressed
And feeling blue,
If something really bothers you,
Turn to someone you can trust.
Talk it out before you bust.

If you're not happy,
Do not pretend,
For somewhere out there is a friend.
Tell them quick what's ailing you,
You'll feel better when you do.

You are special.
This is true!
SOMEONE
Will take care of you!

BALLOONS OF MANY COLORS

Balloons of many colors
Sailing across the sky
As we watch with wonder—
How far will they fly?

Maybe one will land nearby
And take us for a ride
High above the mountain tops
And over oceans wide.

Off to distant countries
To learn a thing or two,
Bringing back ideas—
Think what we could do!

A better understanding
Of cultures old and new,
Sharing all our knowledge:
A better me and you!

SUNSET AND SUNRISE

Sunset and sunrise
Are nature's paintings in the sky.
Golden hues warm the day
And then add color to the night.

Let's admire nature's art;
Appreciate it with delight.
For every day there's something new
Painted fresh for me and you.

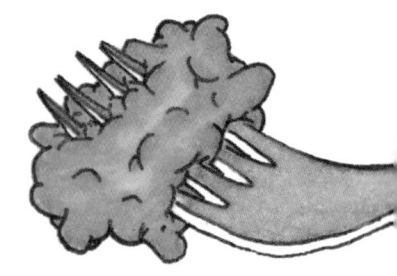

WHAT'S THIS GREEN THING?

Eat your spinach! Eat your peas!
"No!" said Vanessa. "Because they're green!"
She'd examine her food;
She'd look very close.
If she saw something green,
She'd turn up her nose.
No lettuce on her sandwich,
No broccoli on her dish;
Green beans and green peppers
Would never touch those lips.
Parsley. Basil. Oregano.

Would she try these spices?
NO!   NO!   NO!
Then, on Thanksgiving,
Her eyes full of glee,
"GUESS WHAT?" she said,
As she ran up to me.
"What now," I thought,
"What could it be?"
"I ATE SOMETHING GREEN!"
She shouted to me.

ONE OF A KIND

We all have certain talents.
Seek and you shall find
Traits that make you special;
We're all one of a kind!

And when you know your talents,
Use them as you can.
It just might bring you happiness
And help your fellow man!

MY FRIEND DEE

I have a friend whose name is Dee,
And people claim she's a lot like me!

We play with trains and cars and boats.
If I'm the player, she's the coach.
We hunt for insects, rocks, and marbles;
We love to cause our sisters trouble!
When we grow up, me and Dee,
We'll still be friends—
I GUARANTEE!!!

BROTHERS!

I'm sick of my brother;
Please send him to Mars!
Go make the arrangements,
Regardless of charge!

He's always a pain
And gets in my way.
He drives me insane
Twenty-four hours a day!

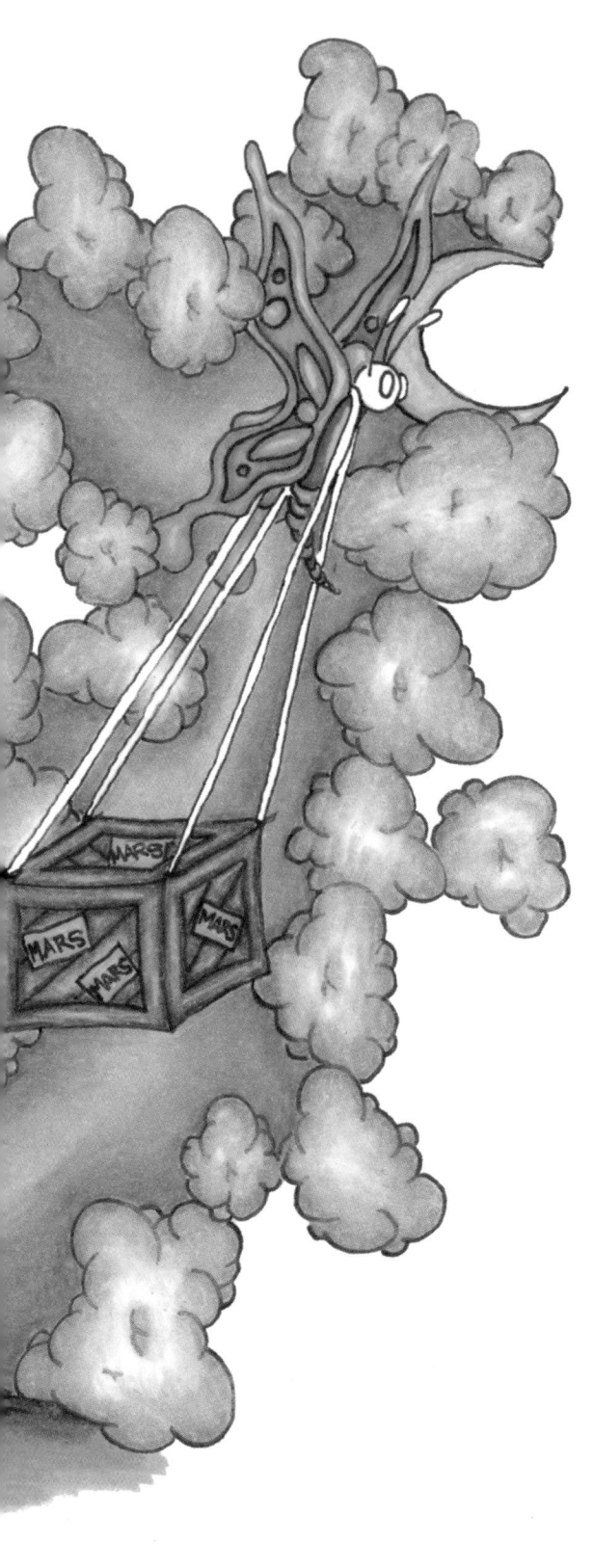

WE

Don't see color;
Don't see race.
It's not the enemy;
It's just a face.

It's not *you*;
It's not *me*.
It's something stronger:
It's called *we*!

We are not black;
We are not white.
We're human beings
With equal rights.

We must not fight.
We must not hate.
Let's all unite.
Let's tolerate!

STELLA'S DILEMMA

Cousin Stella had a dilemma
That caused her much dismay.
A winter storm passed through her town,
Which caused the mayor to say:
"We regret to announce a major delay,
But none of our phones will be working today."
Stella groaned and shed a tear.
Her parents gave a shout and a cheer!
And——
Her brothers yelled, "MAN THIS IS HEAVEN!"
For Stella's had a phone attached to her ear
Since June——of 1987!!

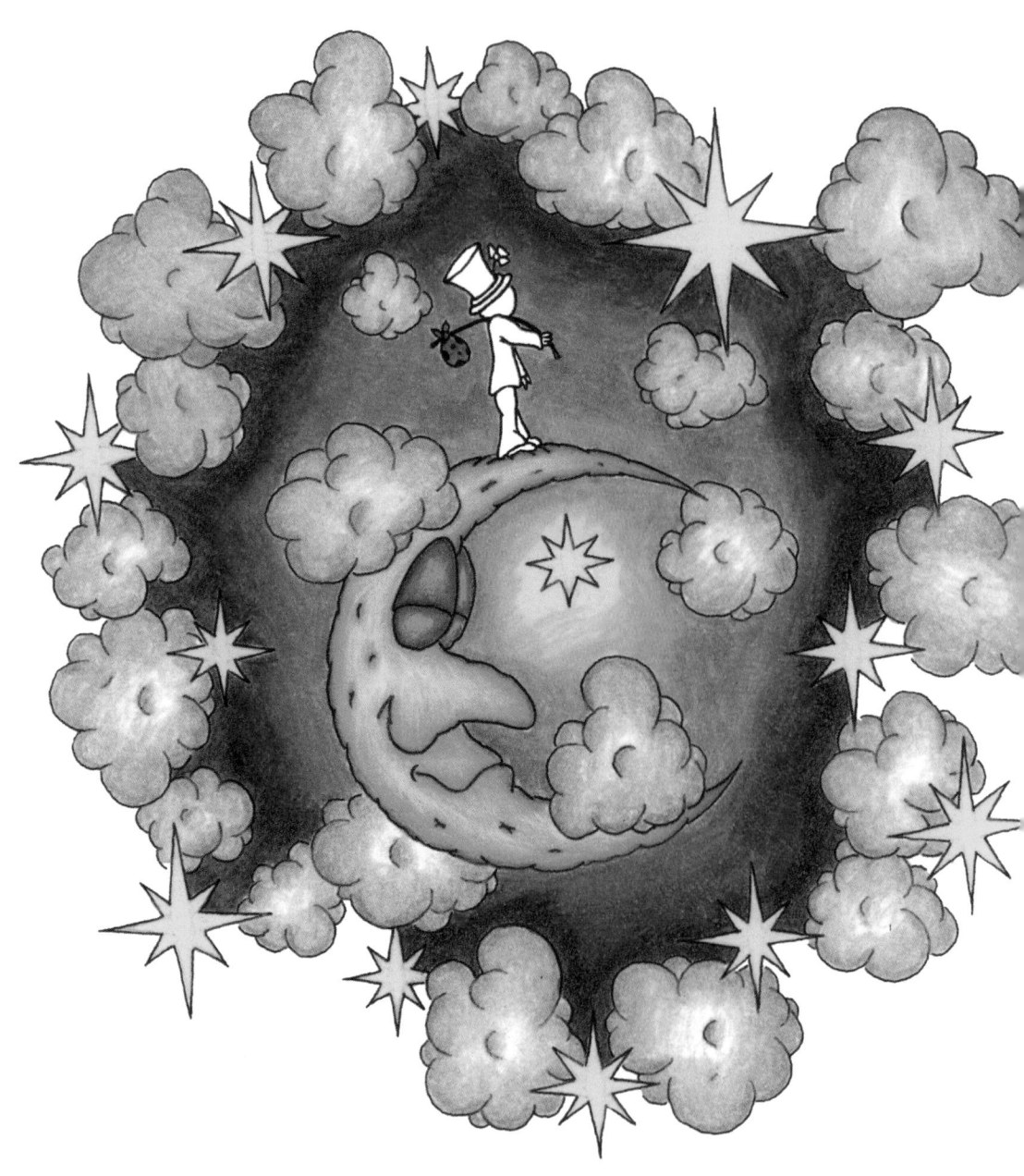

DIFFERENCES

Did you ever wish upon a star
And gaze upon it from afar
Or feel inside how lucky you are?

Can you hear the robins sing
And the phone, when it rings,
Or do you rely on other senses to hear things?

Did you walk or run today
And move obstacles in the way,
Or do you need help to move around okay?

How do you greet the people you know?
Do you sign, shake hands, or bow down low,
Or do you simply say "Hello"?

Have you ever been really sick
But gotten better pretty quick,
Or have you an illness you can't quite lick?

If everyone was just alike, wouldn't it be boring?
Take all the differences and learn.
Now that would be rewarding!

A FAMILY DINNER

Mashed potatoes
(In our soup)
Mustard
(For our peas)
Peanut butter
(With our meat)
Garlic
(On our cheese)

I didn't need a recipe.
(I thought of this myself!)
Who said I couldn't do it?
(Who said I needed help?)

"Please come and eat," I proudly say.
(I'm eager, now, you see.)
"What do you think of dinner?"
(What do you think of me?)

LOLLIPOPS

If you cannot sleep at night,
Try to count some lollipops!
Orange, cherry, grape, or lime,
You will have a good ol' time.
Count them fast or count them slow,
Makes no difference how they go.
Any shape or any size,
Make them thin or make them wide.
This will help you fall asleep
More easily than counting sheep!

CHRISTMAS AND HANUKKAH

It's Christmastime for Dax and Bea.
They'll sing carols around the tree!

It's Hanukkah for Neal and Lauren.
They'll say prayers and light the menorah!

Different customs, different traditions;
Similar thoughts, similar wishes!

SNOWFLAKES

Snowflakes falling to the ground,
Swirling, twirling, all around,
Never making any sound——
Wintertime is here.

Everything is turning white,
Creating such an awesome sight.
I hope it snows throughout the night——
Wintertime is here.

Let's go out and have some fun;
We'll catch snowflakes on our tongues.
My favorite season's now begun——
Wintertime is here.

Making footprints as we go,
Making angels in the snow,
Making snowballs we can throw——
Wintertime is here.

NO TV?

This is weird and so absurd,
The craziest thing I've ever heard.
My parents made a bet with me:
Can I exist without TV?
Feeling brave, I said I'd try;
But underneath, I thought I'd die!
This meant finding things to do—
Is there life without the tube?

The library will see more of me,
I'm sure of this, most definitely!
I'll rediscover the great outdoors,
Take long walks, and exercise more.
I won't rush through anything.
This is sounding interesting!
Lots of time for family and friends,
This doesn't have to be the end.

It might just work, this no TV—
Will I survive? We'll have to see!

STORY TIME

Please read me a story
So I can see
If others live
Like you and me.

Please read me a story
So I can learn
About insects or flowers
Or why the earth turns.

Please read me a story
So I can laugh.
It'll make up
For the bad day I've had.

Please read me a story—
Any one will do.
I treasure time
Spent alone with you!